FEB   2012

Can you Tell a Horse from a Pony?

Buffy Silverman

Lerner Publications Company
Minneapolis

Lerner Publications Company
A division of Lerner Publishing Group, Inc.
241 First Avenue North
Minneapolis, MN 55401 U.S.A.

Website address: www.lernerbooks.com

Library of Congress Cataloging-in-Publication Data

Silverman, Buffy.
      Can you tell a horse from a pony? / by Buffy Silverman.
          p.   cm. — (Lightning bolt books™— Animal look-alikes)
      Includes index.
      ISBN 978-0-7613-6740-6 (lib. bdg. : alk. paper)
          1. Horses—Juvenile literature. 2. Ponies—Juvenile literature. I. Title.
      SF302.S56 2012
      636.1—dc23   2011024588

Manufactured in the United States of America

1 — CG — 12/31/11

Table of Contents

Long or Short Legs?

Horses and ponies look a lot alike. They both have manes. A mane is the long hair that covers the neck of a horse or a pony.

Can you guess which of these animals is a horse and which is a pony?

Their tails also have long hair. Both horses and ponies swish their tails to chase flies away.

This horse swishes its tail as it feeds on grass.

But you can tell horses and ponies apart. Ponies have short, strong legs. They help ponies pull heavy carts. They let ponies run over rocky ground.

This Norwegian Dun pony pulls a cart of hay.

A horse has longer legs.
It stands tall. A horse gallops
and races on its long legs.

How Many Hands?

How do people measure a horse or a pony? They use hands! One hand equals 4 inches (10 centimeters).

People measure horses from the ground to the withers. The withers is the highest part of a horse's or a pony's back.

This tall animal is a horse. Adult horses are fourteen and a half hands or taller. That means they are at least 58 inches (147 cm) tall.

The shire horse is the tallest kind of horse.

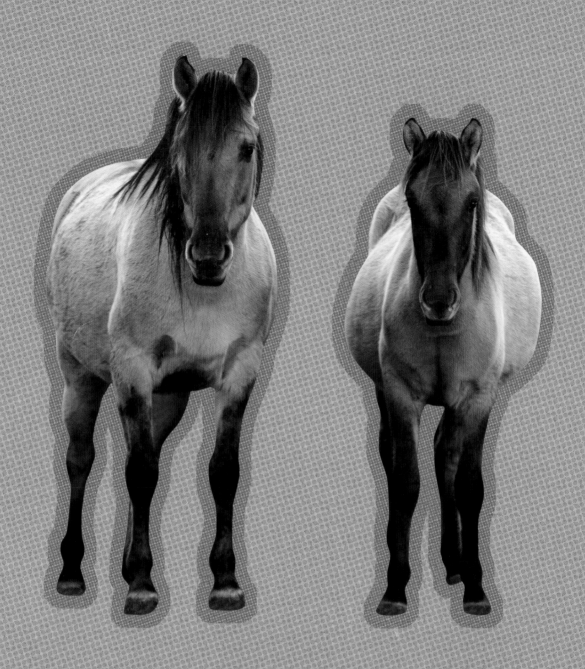

Ponies are shorter than horses. Their bodies are wider. Adult ponies are less than fourteen and a half hands tall.

A miniature horse is even shorter than many ponies. But it doesn't look like a pony. It looks like a tiny horse. Do you see this miniature horse's long legs?

This miniature horse named Einstein weighed only 6 pounds (2.7 kilograms) at birth.

Living with People

Horses have lived with people for thousands of years. They've helped farmers plow fields. Horses have pulled heavy loads. And horses have carried travelers.

These horses pull a carriage carrying President Woodrow Wilson (back left) in 1915.

Some people took horses to dry, rocky places. These horses found less grass to eat. The horses needed short, strong legs to climb over rocks. Over time, they became smaller and tougher. These animals are modern-day ponies.

A Shetland pony roams the land in 1934.

Ponies often lived in windy, cold places. They grew thick fur to keep warm. Most ponies have thicker manes, tails, and coats than horses.

This pony's thick fur keeps it warm in the snow.

Some horses lived in warm, wet places. They found plenty of grass to eat. They grew taller. They did not need thick fur. That's why most horses have thinner manes, tails, and coats than ponies.

Long ago, some people bred special horses to help them do their work. Tall, heavy horses plowed fields. They pulled large wagons. These big, strong horses are called draft horses.

These draft horses plow farmland.

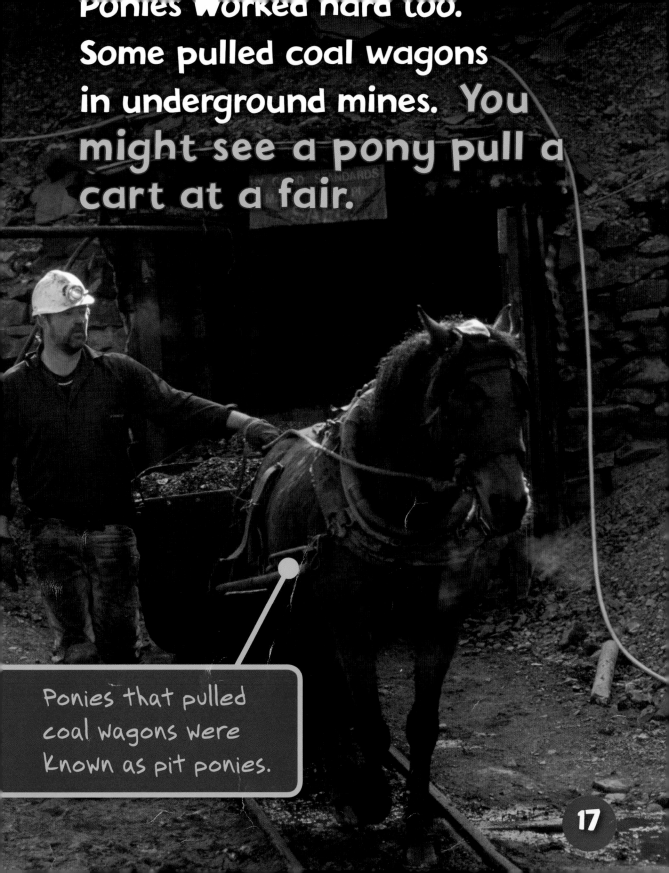

Ponies worked hard too. Some pulled coal wagons in underground mines. You might see a pony pull a cart at a fair.

Ponies that pulled coal wagons were known as pit ponies.

Some people bred horses to run fast. Horses with strong legs can run and jump. People rode them when they hunted. Some people still ride horses for certain kinds of hunting. People also race fast horses.

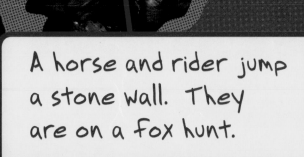

A horse and rider jump a stone wall. They are on a fox hunt.

Staying Safe

Look at this horse's long head. Large eyes are on the sides of its head. A horse can see in all directions. Horses stay alert.

A pony has a shorter head.

Its large eyes can spot danger.
Its ears can hear very quiet
sounds. A pony can smell
scents from far away.

Long ago, horses were wild animals. They did not live with people. They stayed safe by living in large groups called herds. They watched and listened for danger.

A type of horse called a Przewalski's horse still travels in herds. It's the only kind of horse that has never lived with people. Przewalski's horses live in central Asia. There, they eat grass, fruit, bark, and leaves.

A Przewalski's horse has short legs and a short neck, like a pony.

Wild Horses and Ponies

Sometimes horses escape to the wild. They live together in herds. They find their own food and water. Wild horses survive without help from people.

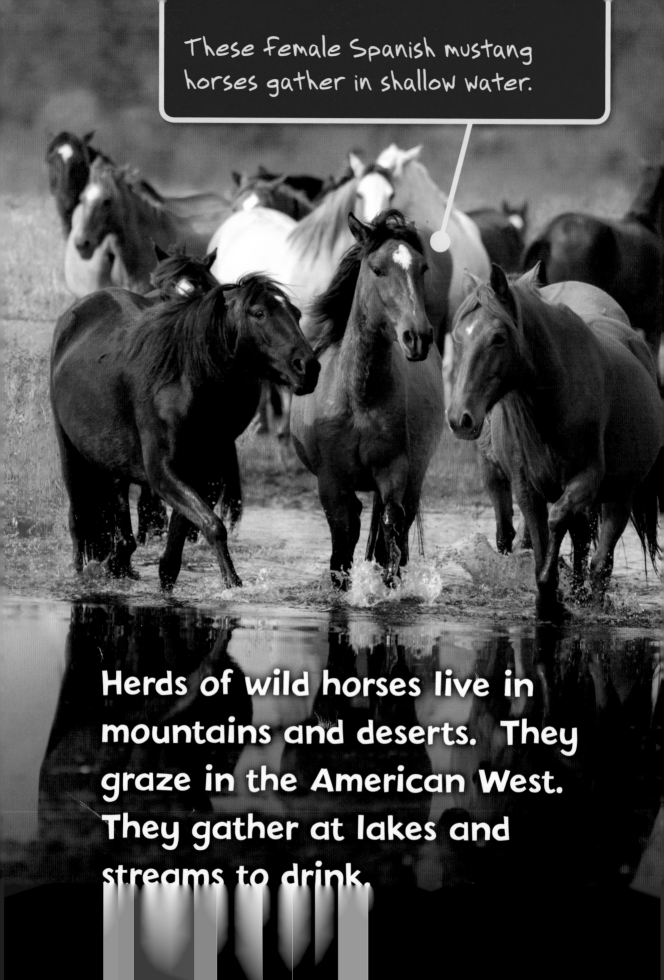

These female Spanish mustang horses gather in shallow water.

Herds of wild horses live in mountains and deserts. They graze in the American West. They gather at lakes and streams to drink.

A herd of wild ponies lives on Assateague Island in Maryland. Farmers brought horses to the island more than three hundred years ago. The modern-day herd of ponies came from these animals.

Wild ponies graze on Assateague Island.

In summer, the wild ponies graze on the beach. The breeze off the water keeps biting flies away. Shaggy coats keep the ponies warm in winter.

This wild pony stands on the seashore.

Horses and ponies roam in grassy places.

People ride them for work and fun.

Can you tell these
look-alikes apart?

Who Am I?

Look at the pictures below. Which ones are horses? Which ones are ponies?

I race on long, strong legs.

My short, strong legs let me pull heavy carts.

My thick fur keeps me warm and dry.

I stay cool with a thin coat and mane.

My short head rests on my short, thick neck.

My long head rests on my long neck.

Answers:
column 1: horse, pony, pony; column 2: pony, horse, horse

Fun Facts

- You've probably seen many breeds of dogs and cats. There are hundreds of breeds of horses and ponies too.

- Shetland ponies are one of the smallest breeds. Some of these small ponies have a special job. They are trained as guides to help blind people.

- Shire horses are one of the largest breeds. They measure seventeen hands or taller. Shire horses are often taller than the people who own them!

- Thumbelina holds the record as the world's smallest horse. She is four hands tall, or 17 inches (43 cm). She only reaches the shins of other horses.

- In 1860, the pony express delivered the mail in the western United States. But the men who rode in the pony express did not ride ponies. They rode fast horses that carried the mail.

Glossary

bred: chose animals with certain traits to mate and have young

coat: the hair covering the body of a horse or a pony

gallop: to run fast

graze: to feed on grasses and other plants

hand: a unit for measuring horses and ponies. One hand is equal to 4 inches (10 cm).

herd: a group of wild animals that stays together

mane: long hair covering the neck of a horse or a pony

Przewalski's horse: a wild horse of central Asia

wild: living in a natural state. Wild animals are not tame and do not live with people.

Further Reading

Brecke, Nicole, and Patricia M. Stockland. *Horses You Can Draw.* Minneapolis: Millbrook Press, 2010.

Creature Features: Przewalski's Horses
http://kids.nationalgeographic.com/kids/animals/creaturefeature/przewalskis-horse

Horse Printouts
http://www.enchantedlearning.com/subjects/mammals/horse/Horseprintouts.shtml

Landau, Elaine. *Shetland Ponies Are My Favorite!* Minneapolis: Lerner Publications Company, 2012.

Lock, Fiona. *Ponies and Horses.* New York: DK Publishing, 2009.

Momatiuk, Yva, and John Eastcott. *Face to Face with Wild Horses.* Washington, DC: National Geographic, 2009.

Nelson, Robin. *Horses.* Minneapolis: Lerner Publications Company, 2009.

Wild Ponies
http://www.nwf.org/Kids/Ranger-Rick/Animals/Mammals/Wild-Ponies.aspx

Index

Photo Acknowledgments

The images in this book are used with the permission of: © Maryart/Dreamstime.com, p. 1 (bottom); © Fouroaks/Dreamstime.com, p. 1 (top); © Bjakko/Dreamstime.com, pp. 2, 4 (right); © Kunstgalerie Aquarius/Flickr/Getty Images, p. 4 (left); © Writer/Dreamstime.com, p. 5; © Andrew H. Brown/National Geographic/Getty Images, pp. 6, 28 (top/right); © Miltudog/Dreamstime.com, pp. 7, 28 (top/left); © Jens Ressing/dpa/CORBIS, p. 8; © Animals Animals/SuperStock, p. 9; © tbkmedia.de/Alamy, p. 10; AP Photo/Jim Cole, p. 11; The Granger Collection, New York, p. 12; © Shetland Museum Photographic Archive, p. 13; © Redmond Durrell/Alamy, pp. 14, 28 (middle/left); © Cherylcasey/Dreamstime.com, pp. 15, 28 (middle/right); © Allen Russell/Alamy, p. 16; © CountrySideCollection – Homer Sykes/Alamy, p. 17; © Darren Staples/CORBIS, p. 18; © Meggj/Dreamstime.com, pp. 19, 28 (bottom/right); © Life On White/PhotoDisc/Getty Images, pp. 20, 28 (bottom/left); © Leonard McCombe/Time & Life Pictures/Getty Images, p. 21; © Jim Brandenburg/Minden Pictures, p. 22; © Photo 24/Photographer's Choice/Getty Images, p. 23; © Mark J. Barrett/Alamy, p. 24; © Craig Lovell/Eagle Visions Photography/Alamy, p. 25; © Vicki Beaver/Alamy, p. 26; © Pirita/Dreamstime.com, p. 27 (top); © Sandy_maya/Dreamstime.com, p. 27 (bottom); © Isselée/Dreamstime.com, pp. 30, 31.

Front Cover: © Eric Isselée/Shutterstock Images (top); © Sandy Matzen/Dreamstime.com, (bottom).

Main body text set in Johann Light 30/36.